ICED COFFEE IN AN UBER

Written By

RAE

Iced Coffee In An **Uber**

Written by Rae
Copyrights © 2021 by Rae

To my beautiful mother and grandmother being there for me and giving me constant advice and support regardless of what on earth it is I find myself wanting to do, they are always right there and I am forever grateful. Thank you to **my best friend** for telling me to go after my dream of writing when I didn't even believe in it anymore. To the **boys that broke my heart and inspired me** to write a lot of this book in the back of multiple **Uber cars** when I didn't have my own car, I thank you for inspiring me to write more but I also hope your future girlfriends and children read my books and bring me up all the time...

Have a great life, my loves :)

Rae

THE FLAG IN MY HEART

When the morning comes,
It'll all be okay
So wipe your tears,
And continue to pray

Throughout the war,
Regardless of the pain,
Throughout the heavy cries,
Tears like tsunami rains,
Praying and staying hopeful
Had always been what
Has kept me sane

ODE TO A COUNTRY,

In which I had never been
The people, oh how kind
The beautiful music,
The rich culture and tradition.
Why did it stop so suddenly?
Why did all the beauty suddenly
Go hidden?

Why did people
From all over the world
Flock there to do more
Harm than actual good?

To a place, once called home,
Why did the government turn on their people?
How can a country
Kill off their own people?

Ode to a country
In which I had never been
Even throughout all this war,
I still call this country home
In between the heavy rubble,
I still find my hammer of hope;
One by one, step by step,
I would help build it back up.

Do I find it hard to call this place home?
Although I had never been?
No. I really do not.
This place is my home
In the heart.
It may not be now,
But one day, in many ways
It will be built back up
And better than ever.

All it takes is
Heart and soul,
Patience and dedication.

With enough of this,
Soon I see this place being
A new place of euphoria.
Just keep the faith,
Keep the patience
Within this sweet home
That we can all share.

So, Ode to a country
In which I had never been
But will always remain
To call my home
Deep down
Within my heart.

VIBE OUT

I want to vibe-
That San Francisco feel
Going to a local coffee shop
After it rains,
Leaving the mist in the air,
The sun peeking over the thick clouds,
Getting an iced coffee
And taking in the scenery.

AS I SIT AT WORK,

Drinking another iced coffee,
I tap my pen against the desk,
Holding the blank receipt in my hand
Thinking of what to write.

Then I looked at the Polaroid
From the back of my phone case
I instantly feel my heart grow warm.
I remember our hugs, our Eskimo kisses,
Cute picnics we would take
Where we smell the vibrant flowers
And feed the baby squirrels.

I remember the times
We would go ice skating
And I would fall,
Even if I was not hurt,
You would siren off as if you were

An off duty paramedic
And carry me off of the ice,
Whispering sweet songs in my ear.

Then we had to say goodbye,
I held you so closely, listening to
Your beautiful songs you wrote.
Every evening, You told me it would all be okay,
We would meet again in our dreams.

"IT'S OKAY, LOVE. WE WILL SEE EACH OTHER SOON... JUST A FEW MORE MONTHS, LOVE"

So as I sit at work,

Drinking yet again

Another iced coffee,

I think of all our memories;

We share,

Laugh about,

Blush about,

Tear up about,

And I think of what is to come...

I think of the warm feeling I can only discover

From within your arms.

LOOK DEEPER FOR ME

When you asked me to look deeper
I never thought twice,
When you asked me to look deeper,
I looked into your brown eyes-
But that just wasn't enough
I wanted to know all about you
Your past and your goals
Your years of experience, and your future
I wanted to know everything.

When you asked me to look deeper,
I never thought twice,
So I kissed you,
And at that very moment
I felt your world shift,
I felt your heartbeat through the warmth
Of your soft, yet so sharp of breaths you took
Gave me chills
But it still wasn't enough.

When you asked me to look deeper,
I never thought twice
You asked me to sit and think,
Then I felt your soft hands
And listened to you speak.

Every letter of,
Every single word,
Every pronunciations
And every stutter,
Every smile and
Every tear,
You smile from your heart
From your soul,
From the deepest parts of you.

So when you asked me to look deeper,
I never thought twice,
I felt every part of you,
Every single inch, your words as cold as ice
Your heart as warm as
Roasted marshmallows

In the middle of August.
When you asked me to look deeper,
I never thought twice
I have come to the realization
That maybe what I feel for you is even
Deeper within me too.

IT'S ALL IN YOUR HEAD...

Fear has many interpretations
And floods our minds often
In so many different ways.
It's often wanting to see things that are of the
Unknown.

You want to be okay
Even if you already are,
But your fears make you feel
Like so much more is actually wrong.
Your heart beats so fast,

Your hands shake,
Your whole body breaks out into
Cold sweats. **Why?**
You are in fear.
Sometimes you grow more into the fear
Beginning to grow full of panic.

"Why? Why? Why?"

You constantly bang your head
On the wall, trying to figure it out
When you simply cannot.
You can't answer or tell why
You're so scared.
You swore up and down that you were fine

Just a minute ago- and now you're not.
Now your thoughts are
Taking over and you're curled up into a corner,
A corner of your mind-
All alone as your thoughts argue back and forth,
Back and forth.
Then suddenly-it stops.
Then you feel fine, but scared out of your mind.
Then you stop to think,
And suddenly
You realize something;
The feeling of fear
Is all in your head.

WHAT DO I EVEN MEAN TO YOU?

Him: You like someone else?

Her: Yes... Yes I do.

Him: I thought you loved me?

Her: Don't get this twisted, I cannot wait on you for forever like you think I can. I had loved you and I was willing to wait but as the time went on, I had to ask myself... would you have ever done the same for me?

Him: I... I...

Her: Or let me ask you this. If I was sick and you were the only one who could save me, would you ever do that? Would you hesitate or do all you could to help? If your blood could save me, would you give it, or keep it and look away?

Him: What do I mean to you?
What did I ever mean to you?

Her: You once meant the world to me, but now you are just a piece of my broken memories.

Him: So, is that all? You don't love me?

Her: We were never together, I cannot even say we were close in heart because, when I gave you my very own- all you did was let it slip and fall through your hands. Then it broke and bam-

Just like that, you were gone.

Read at 4 : 47 am

TIME IS OF THE ESSENCE

Time is of the essence
You ever take the time
To look into the eyes of another person?
The windows to the soul
The things that show so much about a person
What would you do?
How would you feel if you
Look into the eyes of your father
Someone who promised to always be there for you
And never hurt you,
But he did time and time again-
How would you feel?
What about the eyes of

An officer sworn to protect,
But is only giving you choice between
Life and death-
How would you feel?
Or looking into the eyes
Of a lover who promised to

Always be there, but lied-
How would you feel?
Better yet-
What do you feel when you see things
That may not have been there
In the first place?
That was not there in the past?
Do you do absolutely nothing and pretend
That it was all okay and that you never saw it?

Do you leave the person all alone and never speak
With them ever again?
How is it that we claim to love the people
We have so much history with,
Yet you still at times know

Nothing about the inner them?
The real them, feelings and emotions,
Constant thoughts,
Their own mental state?
How can you not know?
Hmm... that may just be-
The mystery... the mystery behind their eyes,
The mystery locked deep within the depths of their soul.

WHEN YOU'RE IN NATURE,

You just suddenly become one with yourself.
It is almost as if nothing else in the world really matters
No problems matter anymore,
Your mental health becomes so subtle
So calm like the kisses of the sunset on the lake.
The beauty- this is what is really shown.

You begin to notice so much more,
Even if it is just the smallest of things,
That beautiful rose that you walked past every day
You notice that.
The vibrant colors, you notice how graceful
It is as it sways within the wind;
You just begin to take into every detail- it's amazing.

For that very moment,
It could be a day, or it could be a week
Or even a split second-
Something in your heart and something in your soul
It tells you something,
You can really get a message
Even if there's nothing but pure silence.

The whole message is there if you just
LISTEN.

Sometimes we take the smallest things
For granted.
There are times when the beauty
Is all in silence.
Pure
Silence.

THINGS I'VE LEARNED AT 19 YEARS OLD

It's okay to not be okay some days,
Nobody is perfect and we don't
Have one hundred percent perfection
Within each and every day
Sometimes it's good to just sit
And analyze, taking the good with the good,
Letting the rest of it go.

Sometimes you have to
Keep certain things to yourself.
Yes, I get that you are excited
To be doing things

But not everyone is out here
With your best interest in mind
And they definitely do not feed off of you

Being happy and having positivity.
Some people live for you to be miserable,
They feed off of and thrive on
Negativity anywhere they can get it.
Learn to have silence sometimes,
Unfortunately, this becomes necessary
At some point.

People who you once
Were so fond of and never thought
You could live without, can change.
They can become so different than what
They were before.

You cannot let your past
Connect like the Bluetooth in your car,
Syncing to your present,
And disturbing your future.
The past happened in the past,
And it's best to turn that Bluetooth off
And keep it where it belongs.
It's hard sometimes but
You have to learn this.

WHAT THE HELL IS LOVE

To some,
Love is an **emotion**
That we all feel,
And to some, it is an **illusion**
Like Cupid intentionally shooting us with **daggers**
Instead of arrows,
Telling us who we should love.
At some point, you will feel love
To some you will give love but
Please be careful.
People can change,
And the love you have for them
May be hard to break away from.
Be careful who you give that to.

SOCIETY UNTIL TOMORROW.

From a society
Built on teachings that
Friends are only for pretend
There's too many of these countless
Infinite thoughts in my head.
I am terrified that I will be a book
No one wants to read,
A song that everyone forgets the lyrics to,
A genre of music that no one listens to,
I am afraid that I will be a movie
Playing over and over again
In a deserted theater,

But when tomorrow comes,
The bright light will shine
So there is not much more to worry about.

This is not a stop
But it is more of a pause in life.
The things that once corrupted my essence
Are beyond numerous
So this pause is a time of recovery,
Like rehab
For my mental health,
Rehab to save my life from the painful drug
Known as **Anxiety**.

YOUTH IS SOMETHING

Youth is like a never ending maze,
Like being alone in the middle of the sea
Without a life jacket or a paddle.
Youth can be overwhelming
But in your youth,
You fight for what you believe in,
It means finding the true definition
Of friendship.
Youth means
Rebelling,
Youth is going out at
3 in the morning
To buy a milkshake and go on a road trip.

YOUTH IS FREEDOM

We cried so much,
But for as many tears that fell,
There were just as many laughs and giggles,
It is purely beautiful.

Tell me every terrible thing
You did in your youth
And let me love you
For them anyway.

Do not disappear on me,
Our youth is never ending,
Always a piece of us.

Youth is so beautiful,
So let's walk out the door,
And begin to enjoy every moment.

I BARELY KNOW MYSELF

Opening up?
I rarely open up.
In a sense, I actually despise
The feeling of being so
Vulnerable or having the possibility
Of being misunderstood at all.

However, every
Now and then,
I get to talking to someone,
And honestly something about
That person just
Highly resonates with me.

Whether it is a total stranger or
Someone as close to me like my mother,

In their presence
I just feel a certain safety,
An almost rare calming feeling and everything
Just comes gushing out of me.

LET'S TALK

Forget about what is politically correct,
Forget about what is polite,
Let's delve right into what is
Most sincere and honest.
Lead me down into a labyrinth,
Show me your true self,
I am not at all interested in the pleasantries
If you want to have a conversation,
Then grab my hands and hold them
As tightly as you can and let's get lost together.
Texting is a brilliant way
To completely misunderstand
How a person is feeling,
Or to misinterpret other people's words.

My heart knows me
All too well.
The truth is,
I am the type of person,
Of very few
Who actually means it
When I ask what is wrong.
The only problem is,
I have little, to no idea
How on earth
I should respond after that.

I don't know how to make it any better.

But I promise,
I will always listen
Really that is all
I can do it.
Honestly on the real,
The oddest of the oddest things
Can hurt me.
These things get stuck in my head
And they are constantly
Playing.
I just overthink a lot,
And it screws up way too much
That at times, never happened
In the very first place.

WORDS ONLY HURT LIKE A BEE STING

A thing about me
Is if you yell at me
Or were to insult me,
I will be wounded for a while.

When I was a child,
I was the type to
Hardly ever misbehave-
I guess you can call it
A Ms. Goody Two Shoes.
I could have never stood
To have had an adult scold me.

Even if a teacher
Disciplines someone next to me,
I would feel the tension in me,

Rippling through my veins so much so,
That you would think
I am the one being
Punished.
I rethink many things
Time and time again
On a daily basis.

I replay your words,
And reply with my very own
As well as feeling the emotions
I felt with it,
Even the ones I wanted to feel.

THE GIRL WITH THE PEN

This is how I analyze and assign
The meaning of things that happen every day.
Writing,
And writing,
And writing even more.
More thoughts
Vividly dancing across each page.
As I erase,
Tear paper up,
Spilling ink all over my lap, drawing up the vivid
Imagery in my head, attempting
To delete them from my mind
Once and for all.

Onto a canvas
Is where my tragedies slowly

But surely
Become beauties.

The utter thoughts
In which I had merely presumed
Non-existent, almost extinct, I guess
In all actuality were

Always there.

So now,
I must ask a true,
Idealistic question not just to myself,
Physically, but my mind
My soul,
My heart.

"Did it get better?
Or did I just make a better mask
To hide it all?"

LOVE AIN'T A THING

I have come to realize that
Love cannot at all exist
Without fear.

The fear of losing you,
Saying the wrong things,
Accidentally hurting or
Disappointing you.
It is all so scary…

Honestly, if I did not
Have this kind of fear,
I don't really care for you.

You mean far more to me
Than you will ever know,
One smile may not be able
To change the world,

But I can say your smile
Changes my whole perspective.
I am never going to sit here and promise
That I can fix all of your problems,
But I do guarantee that you will not
Ever have to face them alone ever again.

You are the most beautiful thing
That I keep within my heart.
I still remember that feeling
Of the first time
I ever talked to you.

God, it was breathtaking...
That amazing smile of yours,
Your innocent cerulean eyes
And the way that they gloss over when you speak,
That soft hair that I could play in for hours,
Just everything about you,
Is so alluring.

Even if you don't see the good in yourself,

Let me show you.
If you ever need a shoulder to lean on,
Let me be the one.

Could this
Be a feeling of love?
I'm not so sure of this.
It is bordering on liking and loving you.
Even on the bad days,
I will still be happy with you.
Honestly even if we can't be together,
I will still be so glad
That you are a part of my life.

FOR MY GIRLS IN THE FRONT

To all of my girls,
A snapchat streak
Does not mean he loves you.
Heart eyes under your photos
On Instagram
Does not show proof
That he loves you,
Neither do **smirks in the hallway.**

Stop waiting for those
4 am text messages and replies
From hours before,
That does not prove that
He loves you, and you know that.

If he loves you only when
Nobody else is around,
Only when he's scrolled through his
Contact list and no one else
Has time for his weak ass,
Stop thinking he must care for you,
Because he just does not.

But picking you up after a long day

Just to talk to you
Is proof that he loves you.
Staying up late after school and practice
Or staying up after hours of work,
Shows he cares for you.

Looking at you
The way in which no one has
Because he can't imagine anyone else
By his side, shows that he cares.

Coming to the door
To talk to your parents

As he waits for you,
Shows that he cares for you.
Opening the door for you
Is a sign of caring,
Not just a single notification
On your phone.
It's the little actions,
Not meaningless booty call hour messages.

Love is a feeling,
And a way of life,
Something this era has seemingly
Changed around.
Listen your gut, ladies.
If something feels off,
It more than likely is.

HONESTY SAVES TIME

If you don't remember anything else,
Just remember to follow your dreams,
Follow your intuition.
Know you are worth far more
Then small replies to late messages.
Believe that.
Love yourself first.
Being happy is a very personal thing,
It honestly has not a thing
To do with anyone else,
Just saying.

A COLOR

Consider yourself to be
A color.
You may not be a real
Favorite to everyone,
Or much of anyone
You want it to be,
But eventually you will find
That artist that needs to finish
Their masterpiece.

"WHY DO I FEEL THIS WAY ?"

Surprise!
Feelings
Are never really going
To make any sense.

Sure, they will make you confused
They drive you halfway up a wall
Then right back down again
For hours at a time
Until it drops you back down
To where you started.

IT'S ONLY YOU

I would just like to tell you
It is you that makes my eyes
Twinkle, smile brighter than a photo.
When I see you,

My heart does a bit of a tap dance
I just get into a calm and happy state
In which I am not sure will be able
To express with words.

I basically turned out to like you
More than I had originally thought-

But another thing
I have seen is that the
More feelings you grow for a person,
So does that feeling of a fear of losing them.

TRUST ISSUES

Well it is not that I don't trust anyone,
I won't even lead a soul into thinking
I am with that kind of persona
But I will say that it is best not to
Instill all of your trust into someone.
They will easily break your heart and leave you
Completely in pieces.
Go in with little to no trust at all,
And have them willingly build your trust,
Build it up on their own.
It will not be easy
But if they really care, they will do it
Slowly but surely.

Trust me, you can
Tell when people
Want or don't want you around at all
Life is too short to tolerate things
Or tolerate people that
Do not make you happy.

LEFT ON DELIVERED
AT 2:25

Is it wild to anyone

Just how faster replies

Make you think the person

Wants to talk,

But the slower replies make you think

You've annoyed the person or

The person found someone better to talk to?

No? Just me?

Okay.

FORGIVE, BUT NEVER FORGET

I did not forgive you out of pure love
It sure as hell wasn't mercy
Because I have none for you, so that's cancelled.
It was definitely not out of sympathy, either
I did forgive you, though
I knew I would need to be forgiven by someone-
A person like me.

Even then, if I kept my forgiveness
To myself- in the future, then maybe
That person... someone like me would also
Keep their forgiveness to themselves and it
Would absolutely kill me.

KINDNESS, A WORD.

A word that is deemed so simple,

How plain this word can be has all an impact

So great.

I first saw the eight letter word in the warm eyes

Of my calm and caring mother.

The other times I began to see it,

I do not remember but I do know

That I looked for it-

In my own eyes,

Within myself.

"HOW DO YOU DO THAT THING WITH YOUR WORDS?

I remember
Sitting in a café somewhere in Ann Arbor,
As I sipped another iced coffee,
You asked me how I did this thing
With my words.
You asked me how I used all these long,
Big and beautiful sounding words
Turning blank pages
Into beautiful tragedies kissed by cursive.
You asked me how it sounds ever so
Eloquent, so fanciful
Coming from out of my mouth.

Well in all actuality, the real truth is
I never really **"did anything with my words"**.
I brought my tears-

The tsunamis and the earthquakes,
The blood lost,
From the slits that rested nicely on my arm
In twisted masterpieces smiling back at me,
In my tangled mind.
The regret and the revenge,
Love and the heartbreak onto a
Blank canvas.
Not actually realizing
That it all came together, and looked like art.

THE THINGS WORDS DO

Words truly
Capture me in lifelong embraces.

How a string of carefully
Picked characters, letters can
Magically bind themselves together
All to form an intimate connection
With the reader, it's so
Intriguing to me.
How these mere sentences can
Cause not just ripples
But tides of change are amazing.

One can do everything
From altering people's perspectives
To making them smile their open,
Slanted smiles that resonated for the quiet
Privacy of their own rooms
When all of their defenses are all
Down with the shortest or longest
Of paragraphs.

There is an infinite amount
Of words
In this universe.

Each of us
As people,
Given a limited quantity
Owing to which all we are
Able to see and feel, and make others
Is restricted.

I want more words
Then just my given share.
I want more words
I want my words to fascinate others
I want to make people wonder about them
For days on end.

LIGHTNING BOLT HEART

With this thunder in your heart

And the melancholy in the art

There is something, utterly

Completely and totally satisfyingly

Perfect about words.

The way they can change lives

In this imperfect and unpredictable life

We all live

It is beyond fascinating.

THE MORNING YOU LEFT MY SHEETS

I know what you think in the morning

When the sun shines on the ground

And shows what you've done.

It shows the places

Your mind has gone,

You swear to your parents that

It will never happen like that again,

But I know what that means.

Yep,

I know.

OUR FEARS

We are not afraid of the dark,
We are afraid of the things
That hides within it.
We are not scared of heights
We are scared of falling to our death.
So within the same instance
You are not scared of loving someone
Or falling in love
You are afraid of being
Rejected.
The possibility of being
Heartbroken again,

The fear of being laughed at again,
You aren't scared of love,
But it's the fear of not being loved back.

You feel as if there
Is no need to go
Through that kind of pain again,
So you try
Your very best not to.

Really, you are not afraid
Of trying again,
You are for the most part,
Afraid of getting hurt for the same exact thing.

NOT MINE TO KEEP.

I am not interested in
These little flings or immature relationships
With guys who want me to
Stroke their egos to make them
Really feel like someone important
In such way that they feel
The need to hurt or belittle others
In the very process.

With you,
I only want new, full bonded
Full blooded connection.

I want to share a bond of love,
And a bond of passion and
Breathtaking adventure.
After all, at the end
Of the day, love is not a past time
But more of a magnificent privilege.

I fled, forgave
And forgot people
As for this hurricane within me
Could either ruin all of them
Or save all of me.
I chose me.

"I JUST FELL OUT OF LOVE WITH YOU"

If you are ever told
That someone fell out of love,
Do a favor for me and do not
Believe them.

You cannot stop loving a community
That once gave you a home,
A city that gave
New adventure every night and morning,
You cannot fall out of love
With the people who set a
Foundation for you
From birth and have been there since.

People cannot stop loving words
That taught them how
To have strength to rise up
From the grounds of ashes.

If you are ever told so,
Tell them that they had never
Stopped loving,
They had just coped up
With circumstances that they had
Originally took away that love in the first place.

FAKER THAN A HUNDRED DOLLAR BILL

I can never do or deal with
Fakeness.
You may not like
And you may not agree
With the things I have to say all the time
But I will make it known where exactly
You stand with me.

If my actions tell you
That I like you,
Then believe that because
I am not acting at all.

One thing you will quickly find out
About me is that
I try to always be
A genuine person.
Sure, I never claimed that it
Has always been this way,
But people are like flowers,
When they learn-
They grow.

A concept in which I just never understood is
being nice to someone in their faces
Only to go talk about them behind their backs.

I also never really understood
Not being forthcoming and
Upfront about your feelings
About other people.
I don't understand
Just how people's words
And their actions
Could not match or add up.
For me,
There is no exact compromise.

If you are an important person to me,
Then I will be loyal
To a fault, and if you're not then
I just won't.
I also expect the same,
If you can't give me the main thing,
Something as simple as respect,
Then evidently I am not a right fit
For a person to be in your life,
And that is perfectly fine with me.

Life is very short and
I have got less than no time
To second guess where I stand
With anyone.
I do not have any time
To worry that people in my circle,
Do not have my best intentions at heart.
If I have to question where I stand with you,
I would think it is best to not have you
Stand with me at all.

ONLY IN MY MIND

Yes, I know
I am a bit quiet,
And I know I do not share
A lot of what is going on in
My mind.
You can believe that
It's not because I am suddenly
Afraid to.
Frankly, I often don't
Find a real person to be able to.
I do not share every
Single thought that crosses my mind
Because, I often know better

Than to believe every thought
That crosses my mind because
I know better than to believe every thought
That was to cross my mind.

I am human, me,
I need to take my time.
Time to observe, analyze, assess
To understand and to correct my own
Thoughts, even before I just let them flow out
Into the world.

I say I need time
Because, I understand
The power of words.
Sure, you are right
I do not speak on thoughts a lot
I definitely do not speak loudly to them.
But at least you know,
That when I do speak
It will be something in which
I genuinely understand,

Something that really excites me
That I believe actually matters
And something that completely feels
True.
Down to my
Soul.
Because to me-
That is generally what speaking
Is really for.

HOW MUCH
I LOVED YOU.

You big idiot,
I would sit for hours on end
Talking about you with
A whole new perspective,
A calm and overly happy state
And even then,
I still wouldn't ever grow tired.

You know I would
Do anything for you and
Honestly, I probably
Still would to this very day.

But the real question is-
Would you ever do the same thing
For me?
You, all you did for me
Was left me lonely, lonely in
My very own thoughts
At night, wondering if I had
Said the right things,
Hoping I did not hurt you.
I used to stay up at night
To wait on your replies,

Totally contradicting my innermost
Thoughts at times.

At the end of the day,
I realize more as time goes on,
You are who I care for, way more
Than I had originally thought,
But the real question is,
Would you ever feel the same?
Would you ever do the same?
Would you sit with me or leave me alone
In the rain?
What do I mean to you?
Am I just your hype person,
Or do you actually care about me?

Tell me.
Don't be scared.
Take a risk, come up to me
Take me to the side,
Call me, Video message me
If you're shy.
But do tell me the
Truth.

I would rather
Be crushed with the truth,
Then be comforted with lies.
Are you playing with my feelings?
Because I seem like the gullible type?

Even if you are playing me,
I still cannot hate you.

That takes way too much energy
Even for the shallowest kinds of people.
I won't speak badly
About you either because,
I surely was not doing that
When I cared for you,
Or was on Cloud 9
Crushing on you.
No need to switch up
So suddenly, like that.

You'd never see me
Angry over you, at all.
My mind will not be
Altered by the amateurish actions
Of someone else.
Why be mad at someone?
Why be mad?
For the sake of yourself,
You come first in any situation
And those are the facts.

SOMETIMES I THINK.

I really wonder,

If a person does not like you,

If they already know they are not

Interested in the very first place,

Why would they start to speak with you?

If your intention is only to leave,

Why begin the story

In the first place?

DISSAPPOINTED BUT NEVER SURPRISED

I can safely say
That I learned my lesson.
You really disappointed me,
That's all.
In the end,
I will be okay.
I will still live my life,
You are not interrupting what is
To come in my future.

IMPERFECTION

Sometimes, evil and cruel people
Need a little extra love,
But don't know how to ask for it.
We as humans are wired for imperfection.
We are wired to have bad days,
Flaws and mistakes,
But that does not mean that we
Cannot be loving, kind, forgiving and enjoying.
No life, no soul
Is perfect.
Nobody has it perfect.
You never know what goes on
Behind closed doors,

Some people actually
Do put up the most believable,
Toughest fronts for the eyes of others.
In all reality,
They are slowly crumbling,
Fading away.

Make sure you extend a hand
For those who need it,
Even if they do not ask for it,
Be observant and be considerate
On the real,
It could save a person's life.

NO ONE AT ALL

No one's going to
Fight for you
As hard as you will fight
For yourself.
Sometimes you gotta have
The positivity flow
Through you and change
Your entire perspective around.
True, nobody ever said it will be
An easy task but over time,
Through this gradual process,
You will begin not only seeing physical
Changes, but you will begin to feel them
In your emotional, mental health state as well.

3 : 23 AM

So, a thought just hit me-

What are you supposed to do?

With the love that is never accepted?

Do you drop it in a box

To keep underneath your bed,

Only to open when you're alone?

Is it just dropped?

Is it continuously just as pure or

Does it belong on the side of the road

Where all of the other dead things lie?

HAVEN'T I LEARNED MY LESSON?

I find myself to be
Quite nostalgic for things
That I am not the slightest of sure
They even exist,
But I still mess with them,
Anyways.

ANXIETY

When I look back on
Just how horrible my anxiety was
Even a couple years ago,
If I could have very few
Words to describe my anxiety
Or anxiety, in general is
"I'm surprised I didn't die at 15",
Or,
I would say that it is a
Hand gripping tightly around
Your neck, making it so you
Cannot breathe,

You cannot speak, you just have to
Look around and watch everyone
Seeing you struggle, but do nothing at all
To help you, more so out of fear
That they may become stuck like you.

No one pries
This hand away from your neck
Or tells you to breathe again.
You're just left wriggling around
Until that hand eventually decides it is time
To drop off of you.

Then when you are finally able to breathe,
It's almost as if you held your breath
For thirty minutes, and are trying to recover.
You have to teach yourself all over again,
And constantly remind yourself
To always keep breathing.
Don't stop
Breathing.

"YOUR EYES FOREVER INTOXICATE ME"

Have you ever taken a
Look at hazel eyes
In the sun?
Sure you may not always
Notice the biggest things at first,
But you'll soon see that hazel
Just does not always describe them.
They slowly melt within the warm
Golden rays, but look so close
To a warm spring day on the beach.

There is no such word as boring,
When you see something as rare
As a person with hazel eyes, no matter
How long you stare at them,
Even hours later- they just turn into
Such a paragon on their own
That you just can't explain.

BE POETIC

If you find the way
The light falls delicately
Through your window, and onto your
Bedroom wall ever so magnificent,
Bringing you pure opportunistic smelling air,
Then go ahead and write about it!
Compare the soft and golden glow to
A fresh honeycomb sitting
In the morning light of the woods.

If poetry is something that
Makes you feel glad to be alive,
I see no way that is silly.

If sunlight is something that makes you happy,
Don't listen to what others may say about it.
You look for the pure,
The absolute beauty in things, so please
Don't take that for granted.
In fact, be proud of it.
Say that you feel the heavy rain kiss you.
Go on and write about the glow of the moonlight
On tree leaves in your backyard,
As you stare at them from out your window.
The dancing of a thousand lilies on Jeju,
Make your world a magical paradise.
Collect every metaphor and treasure all of them.

DEAR EX-FRIENDS,

If you think I am sulking
Over you,
Watching your snapchat stories,
Liking your photos,
Reading what you have to say-
If you pushed me over, then I most certainly
Am not.

To the ones who did not treat me
Like trash, but we lost connection,
Do not worry.

I will always think at random times
About the great memories that we have shared
I say this because once upon a time,
We were attached at the hip,

Just about inseparable.
Always calling, texting,
Video calling each other,
Then is always the
Could've been or the what-if
Questions.
Everything happens for a reason.

I will always watch the videos of us
Laughing like crazy, or look at all
Of the pictures and think back to all
Of the fun we used to have.
I miss you so much and honestly the worst part is
We cannot stay in contact anymore,
And I cannot see you anymore.

We probably walk past
One another as if
We had never met before,
As if we didn't ever stay up late

Until four in the morning telling secrets
Or have billions of inside jokes together.
I will always thank you
For being my first long term best friend.
All I have now is
The memories I will never forget.
Thank you.

Sincerely,
The girl who is obsessed with iced coffee,
Once your best friend.

THE PART OF YOUR HEART THAT GOD DIDN'T ADD

Throughout life,

You will meet one person

Who is totally not like any other person,

You two can be together consistently,

For hours at a time and never get bored,

You could talk to this person everyday

Talk about anything and everything

And never be tired of each other.

You could tell them things and

It seems that they could never judge you.

Don't ever let them go.

IS IT DIFFERENT ?

At times I find it different,
That I find myself actually praying
I will never lose you.
Meeting you was like
Hearing a song on Spotify,
Knowing I would forever replay it.

Sure, I do admit
There are times when I tried to
Deny the fact that I like you,
But that only made me like you way more,
Now it is more than I
Thought I would.

WE'VE LOST OUR GENUINE YOUTHS

When did we stop?
When did we stop wearing
Light up sneakers,
Or the ones with the tiny wheels?

Since when did going
To bed solve any issues?
Why did people stop learning about
The true definition of love
And instead start to settle for
The mediocre?

When did labels matter more
Than anything else?
Since when did weight determine
If someone would find
Us attractive?
When did weight even determine
Who we are as people?
Why did those tiny little scars stop becoming so
Accidental, and done more
On purpose to feel something?

Who are we, honestly?

You are not a name, height,
Weight, age or gender.
Instead, you are your favorite
Books and song lyrics you
Put in your social media captions.

You are the foods you ate
For breakfast on a Tuesday morning,
You are the person you choose to be.
You are a thousand things you want
But everyone decides
To point out the million things
You are not, that they like.

You are not the area
You are from,
You are not a label given by the amount
Of social status you have.

You are where you are going,
And honestly
I would love
To see you go there too.

RAINDROPS FALL

So serene and so peaceful,

I realize slowly that

This is where my happiness lives.

I notice that

The raindrops are like us.

Each one falls inevitably

At some point,

Sometimes together,

Sometimes one by one

They all tell a story.

None of them fight, even in the thunder,

They still seem to peacefully fall into the flow

Of the window.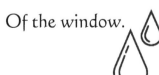

I fIND MY PLACE

Well, actually my soul does
Right between your arms,
Wrapped in your tender kisses
And the soft whispers of the cool spring breeze.
I was in the warmth of your embrace
And the calm scent
Coming from the nape
Of your neck.

Fierceness of your touch,
Our souls have found each other.
Our souls are like Japanese cherry blossoms
On a warm rainy day.
You may not see the small things,
Slowly but surely,
It blossoms.

TWO KINDS OF LOVE

I always thought that there were
Only two kinds of love-
The kind you would **kill for,**
And then the kind of love you would
Die for.

But now,
I know the kind I have;
It is the kind of love
I want to live.
Love sprouted like the flowers,
Grow a beautiful garden
In the mind.

Even on the gloomy days,
The sun will shine.
The rainbow is beautiful to see,
It glows so brightly and
It overpowers all of the sadness
And all the wrongdoings
Of reality.

DATING IS A PARTNERSHIP

It is not an ownership.
Just a little reminder to
Girls out there.
When it comes time for you to date someone,
Choose the guy that will tell you to
Be safe when you go out,
And not get upset about it.

It is two hours from a new year,
There is no way I will
Teach or train another person
How to treat me.
It is either you can act right, or you can get left
Right where I found you.
It is so simple.
Almost 2022 and people

Still cannot be just about one person?
You cannot have one person?

You want to have sides from everywhere?
People can look at the eclipse without glasses,
But not tell their significant other
The truth?

Regardless of age, you deserve the best.
Do not chase after someone
Just because they're is hot
Or just because they might be popular.
Even the most innocent ones
Can still be a heartbreaker,
So watch out for that.
Get to know them.
Do not be so quick to jump
Into a relationship, get to know
Each other, this goes both ways.

NEW LESSONS, HISTORY

We are young and
Make mistakes but be careful.
Keep your mind open with logic.
Keep your mind open
With common sense.
Do not make your heart
Overcome things that feel out of place.
If something feels bad,
Maybe it really is.
Now if I am wrong,
Educate me, but do not
Belittle me.

**If you feel the need
To force something,
Go ahead and leave it alone.**
Whether it is a relationship,
A friendship, or even a conversation
Just go ahead and leave it all alone.
If something is meant to be,
You should never have to question it.
If you think all people will do as you do
For them,
You will forever be disappointed.

"DON'T WASTE PRECIOUS AIR"

You cannot fight someone

On something they actually want to

Believe.

Truth just does not and will not

Register, and logic surely

Will become nonexistent.

The wants will be draped

In nothing but **emotion.**

TONGUE OF GLASS, WORDS FROM A GUN

Sometimes my words
They become a pile of broken glass.
There are also times my words come out
Like bullets.
They do not come out without
Hurting and dripping blood, and sometimes
I forget how to even speak after it.

When I was fourteen,
I was afraid that I was going to
Work myself so hard that I would
End up dying because of it.

I was afraid that everyone would see
That when I told them
I would sleep only when I am dead,
I was never joking.

On the real,
I am so grateful for every chance
I had been given
And I've been given, and
Still am grateful for every second chance.
I am grateful for everyone that thinks about me
And actually shows it.

For everyone that does not think about me
That often, I hope that when I cross your mind
There are good feelings being brought.
For everyone counting on me,
I hope I can make you proud.

EVEN IF YOU DO

Even if you go for it

A hundred times over,

And it still does not work-

Guess what?

You still won.

The fact that you had enough

Guts

And enough

Courage to head into something

That really frightened you,

That is true bravery and it

Will most definitely take you places.

OVERTHINK TO OVERTHOUGHT

Have you ever thought
About something all day long
As to where you feel your eyes burn
Then you begin to overthink even harder?
Honestly it is not like you try to,
But these emotions begin to flow
From out of nowhere.
Your tears slowly fall down your cheeks
And as they dry, they begin to stain your face
Honestly it is the most painful feeling
You just want to scream
And let all of those feelings out

It can be so hard,
So you just put your hand over your mouth,
Close your eyes and let these tears and these fears
Consume you.

IF ONLY THESE FOUR WALLS HAD A VOICE

Over time,
I become paranoid,
Sitting between these four blue walls
Listening to the same tune on repeat
Wondering if my thoughts will ever slow down.

But I have learned that
Silence will not get you anywhere.
It is like being stuck at an automatic door
Refusing to open for you.
I want to scream for help,

But if I break my silence,
Someone will hear me.
Even my whisper is too loud
For my frail mind.
It is in the total silence of nature
Where one finds
Complete bliss.

HONEY BROWN FIRE

A sun that is only burning
In four shades of despair,
Caught somewhere in between
A pair of honey brown eyes,
Did the weight of all days equal up
To another yesterday?
Forgot I had your name to set on fire-
Arson just may become my last name
Instead of your own,
Heart was almost always four steps ahead of me,
Ignited angrier than the rest of us.

So much like June,
The start of our summers
Kneeling down before we go
To leave with something different.
A whole new presence in mind.
They leave with good in their hands.

MORE TIME = ?

I wish people could just
Stop believing that if they had more time,
They would be happier.
Or if they had more money,
They would be happier.
Stop depending your happiness
On things that may occur in the future.
You already have everything you need to make
Every single day count; yourself.
I know that sometimes trying to be happy
Means fighting every single day against
Our inner demons,
While it is easy to not change anything
Deciding to do so is quite difficult.

NOBODY WILL EVER SAY

Nobody will say
Every little thing
That is on their mind ever,
And if they tell you that they do,
Ask them to tell you everything
That is currently on their mind.
Which again brings me back to my own
Original statement.

No one, anywhere
Will share every single thing on their mind,
Or the things in which may
Run through their mind on a daily basis.

People always leave out small bits
A little piece
A secret in which they will
Forever keep.

BITTERSWEET

Life is bittersweet

Sometimes you have to

Take the precious moments and run with them

Because life is the type to throw you

So many curveballs, that all you

Can do is look within the past

For a smile.

Cherish life's good moments and

Keep them deep in your life.

DO IT FOR YOU.

If you want to slit your eyebrow
And dye your hair dark blue,
Go ahead and do that!
Sure you may get a lot of stares,
But you are doing you and this is what
People will salute you for.
If you want to wear sweatpants and
Oversized shirts every day,
Feel free to do that
Without a care in the world.

If you don't care whether your hair is neat or not,
Wear it just how you want to.
Do not listen to society and its
Two faced standards
Because not even the trendsetters these days
Match up to their own standards
That they set.
Only opinion that should be on your mind
Is your very own.

HATE

I despise everyone that
Will come into your life
To love you for the wrong
Reasons, because absolutely
None of them will ever be by your
Side, the way I will.
No one, not one
Of them will ever cheer for you
Or make you feel special,
Be there for you
Just the way you deserve.

STRAIGHT UP

The only thing
I ask for you to do
Is to be straight up with me.
I do not care
If you hurt my feelings,
Just go ahead and do it.
I would be even more hurt
If you did not tell me
The truth,
Especially if you thought
I could not handle it.

I do not need or want you
To sugarcoat every little detail
And to have me read between
The lines.

I had one too many people
In my life like that already, and
The last thing I need
Is a
Plus one.

Even if I seem like
I am not listening to you,
I actually am
And I want you to tell me
What's actually real.
Be real with me, and I will get over it.
It is that simple.

I can safely speak
From perspective in which
I have so closely watched throughout
My late middle school years
Up until now.

The problem that we all
Seemingly face is
Lack of communication.
Nobody is really talking.
Communication is free,
It is face to face
But nowadays it is so rare,
I swear you would believe me
If I say it is almost
Non-existent.

I WONDER

If I will ever be ready
To break out one day and say,
I am ready to be an adult.
Like really, I sincerely wonder
If I can ever be able to pay bills
I wonder if I can ever find a job,
What if I decide to move?
What if I try really hard
To save all of my money…
But I just can't?

Why can't I just be 17
Forever?
What if I can have the mature
Mindset
Of being 17?
The adventurous personality
The travelling spirit?
The girl that falls in love,
And take a flight every other week?
The girl with thousands of Polaroids
Scattered across her room
With memories from holding hands
To feet on dashboards, driving towards
Sunsets?

If I can never be 17 years old again,
If I have to grow and be an adult,
I want to grow to be the adult with
A life I will never forget.
The breeze floats
Ever so gently through my window,
Kissing my cheeks,
The way you did before.

I WANT TO FEEL

That feeling.
Walking through the streets
At two in the morning,
Not knowing where I am even going,

Feeling the warm air,
Seeing the lights of the town
Illuminating each busy street
Full of tourists and natives,
Hearing a language I am not too familiar with,
Falling in love with the scenery every single time.

I don't want Hollywood,
I don't want LA.
I want to go to a place
Where beauty standards don't even matter
Where people don't get famous
For the wrong reasons.
I want to go somewhere
Where judgement is not based on
Your status or if you speak to the
Opposite gender.

I want that free feeling,
I want that 3am excitement,
I want to be free.

HUNGER FOR IT...

I have a hunger,
But not for food.
I have a hunger to make
Things happen.
I have a hunger for
Raw creation and ideas,
A hunger to stay awake
Even until the earliest of the dawn
Writing and working to make things
Better.

I have a hunger for passion,
And I won't stop until
I made it.

It Has Always Been You.
Everything about you
Is what makes me fall madly in love with you
More every single day.
Thousands of miles away
Or right next to each other,
My mind will always
Play the moments of us together.
I love you.

I WANTED IT TO BE US

I always wanted it to be

Just us.

You and I.

Me and you.

Us together.

But I know the kind

Of guy that you are,

The kind of guy you have always been

Towards me.

So in a way,

I just knew that wasn't

Going to happen.

ONLY IN MY DREAMS

My face burns
From the tears
I had saved for the
Quiet nights that I sit,
Wondering if things would ever
Go the way
They do in my
Everlasting evening dreams.

A LETTER TO MY KING.

Oh, how royal we always
Could be.
We dressed each other
In a fountain of silk,
And jewels for years on end.

You held my hands
And we danced so slowly…
As the gazes turned towards us,
For an eternity,
It seemed as if it was just
Us against the world.

God, I miss your touch.
Your presence elevated
My heart.
Just you being there with me
Oh how powerful we were,
The things I would do
To hold your hand again,
To hug you once more,
To wear our crowns once more…
Once more
Together.

WRITER'S BLOCK

Feels so helpless to me.
It's like being in a dark room
With no doors, only a wide window
That allows me to see out,
But nothing can be seen.

Sometimes this block
Feels overwhelming,
Sometimes my anxiety makes me
Think the worst.
This dark room will begin to
Flood.

PART OF MY SOUL THAT I FORGOT

A forgotten piece of
My soul seeping from every corner,
From every crack in the walls,

Getting closer to the window and
Pressing my hands on the cold glass frame,
I see all my ideas on the outside,
Pounding to get into the room to save me,
But they can't.

I honestly don't know
How to get out of the room,
I don't know if I can even try
Finding the light,
I don't know if I can
Find my way, on my own
Out of this cold and soaked room.

THE WEDDING
SHE NEVER WANTED

I sit in this café,
And I tap away at my phone,
Asking myself so quietly
That I'm halfway whispering,
If someone were to walk by, they would
Almost completely assume
I had lost my mind.
I ask why I didn't see things sooner.

I sit in this dimly lit café,
Messaging her,
Hearing her words
Echoing through each
And every text,
Seeing her go from being so happy
To seeing her wither away every single day,
Promising things that she never
Wanted to do, things that are
Too ill-suited to even speak about

In the daylight.
Staring at every photo
As tears rise in my eyes

Seeing nothing but our hands
Yet that told so many stories,
I ask myself why.

I sat at her side and asked
If she was okay,
Seeing her marry someone
Only her family knew,

Seeing her with tears growing quickly
In her eyes,
She grabs my hands
Allows a small smile to cloak
The emotions she was so good at
Hiding.
Emotions that her family told her
Never to have, or show to anyone.
She swore to me, that things
Would be okay.
Why didn't I notice earlier?

In this café
I continued to sit,
Iced coffee after iced coffee,
My wallet seemingly getting thinner,
My napkin that I continue to wipe tears on,
Only getting more and more soaked,
My fingers growing heavier as I type my heart
Into each and every text message to her,
I ask myself **why.**
Why couldn't I have noticed?
Noticed sooner?

HOW DID IT FEEL ?

When you stand in front
Of the mirror,
After overthinking,
Holding in your cries from
Society,
Holding them in from the people
Who you care about enough,
To not let see you cry-
Did it get better?

When you're holding the phone,
After the person who promised
To love you,
Broke your heart-
Did things get better?

When you push things away,
Do they ever really get better?
Or do they just grow to be more
Tolerable?

LOVE OF MYSELF

I knew that in the end,

It was all up to me

To love myself so much more,

In more ways that you never could.

I was not leaving you in the past,

I was not scarring the good we had,

In the past.

But I know I had

To walk towards something

So much better.

PINKY PROMISES AND LIPSTICK STAINS

Can I love you forever ?

Can we sit in a garden of roses?

Can we slow dance as I whisper in your ear,

Telling you how golden brown

Your eyes are

In the sunlight?

Can we have a tea party?

I know it sounds so childish but

With you,

It would make a lifetime.

CAN WE ?

Can we let our
Words
Touch us like the
San Francisco **breeze?**
Can we turn the
Most harmful of words,
Into **masterpieces?**

The damage these words
Have caused,
Can we turn fires
Into **growing gardens?**
Can we turn thunderstorms
Into California sunsets?
Can we turn these cuts
Into pieces of art that lie ever so
Fragile on the strong skin
We have created?

Poetry grows on us.
Nothing in life
That we ever go through,
Will ever come out poetically.
We go through experiences,
And these experiences
Run through our minds

Then we create masterpieces.
The tears we have made,
Were never beauties
In the past.
To us,
It was just always tears.

SATURDAY MORNING IN SAN FRANCISCO

I just want
It to be **Saturday morning,**
In the **spring.**
I want to **vibe**
Harder than ever.

EXPLORE IT FOR ME

I would rather

Explore a person's soul,

A person's mind

And their heart-

Way more than their body

Any time.

Any day.

ICED COFFEE, ENDLESS THOUGHTS, AND A HAPPY DRIVER

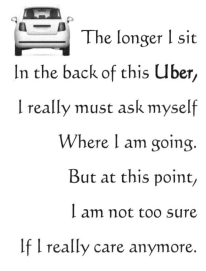 The longer I sit

In the back of this **Uber,**

I really must ask myself

Where I am going.

But at this point,

I am not too sure

If I really care anymore.

So for now,

I will sit

And continue to gaze out this window,

Drinking my iced coffee.

You Are That One Dream

That I Told Myself

To Wake Up From,

But Never Could.

CPSIA information can be obtained
at www.ICGtesting.com
Printed in the USA
LVHW071758200621
690708LV00001B/98